LIVING GREEN

CLOTHING

Information and projects to reduce your environmental footprint

Marshall Cavendish
Benchmark
New York

Helen Whittaker

This edition first published in 2012 in the United States of America by
Marshall Cavendish Benchmark
An imprint of Marshall Cavendish Corporation

Website: www.marshallcavendish.us

This publication represents the opinions and views of the author based on Helen Whittaker's personal experience, knowledge, and research. The information in this book serves as a general guide only. The author and publisher have used their best efforts in preparing this book and disclaim liability rising directly and indirectly from the use and application of this book.

Other Marshall Cavendish Offices:
Marshall Cavendish Ltd. 5th Floor, 32-38 Saffron Hill, London EC1N 8FH, UK • Marshall Cavendish International (Asia) Private Limited, 1 New Industrial Road, Singapore 536196 • Marshall Cavendish International (Thailand) Co Ltd. 253 Asoke, 12th Flr, Sukhumvit 21 Road, Klongtoey Nua, Wattana, Bangkok 10110, Thailand • Marshall Cavendish (Malaysia) Sdn Bhd, Times Subang, Lot 46, Subang Hi-Tech Industrial Park, Batu Tiga, 40000 Shah Alam, Selangor Darul Ehsan, Malaysia

Marshall Cavendish is a trademark of Times Publishing Limited

All websites were available and accurate when this book was sent to press.

Library of Congress Cataloging-in-Publication Data

Whittaker, Helen.
  Clothing / Helen Whittaker.
  p. cm. — (Living Green)
  Includes index.
  Summary: "Discusses how clothing impacts the environment and what you can
do to be more eco-conscious"—Provided by publisher.
  ISBN 978-1-60870-572-6
  1. Clothing and dress—Juvenile literature. 2. Environmentalism—Juvenile
literature. I. Title.
  GT518.W47 2010
  391—dc22
                        2010044337

First published in 2011 by
MACMILLAN EDUCATION AUSTRALIA PTY LTD
15–19 Claremont Street, South Yarra 3141

Visit our website at www.macmillan.com.au or go directly to www.macmillanlibrary.com.au

Associated companies and representatives throughout the world.

Copyright © Macmillan Publishers Australia 2011

Publisher: Carmel Heron
Commissioning Editor: Niki Horin
Managing Editor: Vanessa Lanaway
Editor: Georgina Garner
Proofreader: Helena Newton
Designer: Julie Thompson
Page layout: Julie Thompson
Photo researcher: Claire Armstrong (management: Debbie Gallagher)
Illustrators: Nives Porcellato and Andrew Craig (11); Cat MacInnes (all other illustrations)
Production Controller: Vanessa Johnson

Printed in China

Acknowledgments
The author and publisher are grateful to the following for permission to reproduce copyright material:

Front cover photograph: Girl choosing clothes courtesy of Getty Images/Digital Vision. Front and back cover illustrations by Cat MacInnes.

Photographs courtesy of: Corbis/Ocean, **22** (bottom), /Jose Luis Pelaez, Inc, **5**, /Ariel Skelley, **20**; Getty Images/Digital Vision, **16**, /Ryan McVay, **18** (left); iStockphoto.com/Greg da Silva, **31**, /Bernad Gavril, **3**, **24** (right), /halfshag, **25** (right), /JazzIRT, **12**, /Juanmonino, **15** (left), /mikapp, **7** (bottom left), /thelinke, **9** (bottom), /Jason Todd, **26**; Shutterstock, **10**, /1000 Words, **7** (top), /aborisov, **18** (right), /Akaiser, (environment icons, throughout), /Petrenko Andriy, **17**, /Noam Armonn, **6** (top), **11** (bottom), /Katrina Brown, **4**, **32**, Ivan Cholakov Gostock-dot-net, **11** (aeroplane), /Lucian Coman, **8** (right), /cristi180884, **23**, /Elena Elisseeva, **14** (top), /Faraways, **11** (top), /BW Folsom, **25** (left), /Luisa Fernanda Gonzalez, **8** (left), /gsmad, **30** (middle), /Péter Gudella, **11** (truck), /Kayros Studio, **22** (top), /Laenz, (eco icons, throughout), /mmaxer, **30** (top), /Monkey Business Images, **28** (left), /Thomas M Perkins, **14** (bottom), /Photosani, **24** (left), /PrairieEyes, **9** (top), **15** (right), /Rafael Ramirez Lee, **11** (ship), /sokolovsky, **13**, /Kenneth Sponsler, **11** (train), /Steyno&Stitch, **29**, /vale_t, **6** (bottom), /Stephen VanHorn, **28** (right), /Ye, (recycle logos, throughout), /Yellowj, **7** (bottom right), /Jin Young Lee, **30** (bottom).

While every care has been taken to trace and acknowledge copyright, the publisher tenders their apologies for any accidental infringement where copyright has proved untraceable. They would be pleased to come to a suitable arrangement with the rightful owner in each case.

Please note
At the time of printing, the Internet addresses appearing in this book were correct. Owing to the dynamic nature of the Internet, however, we cannot guarantee that all these addresses will remain correct.

1 3 5 6 4 2

Contents

Transform a toothbrush into wearable art! page 24

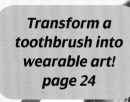

Put more green in your clean! page 28

Glossary Words

When a word is printed in **bold**, you can look up its meaning in the Glossary on page 31.

Living Green

Living green means choosing to care for the **environment** by living in a sustainable way.

Living Sustainably

Living sustainably means living in a way that protects Earth. Someone who lives sustainably avoids damaging the environment or wasting resources so that Earth can continue to provide a home for people in the future.

You and your friends can change your habits and behavior to help Earth. Living green makes sense!

How Our Actions Affect the Environment

Human activities use up Earth's **natural resources** and damage the environment. Some natural resources are **renewable**, such as wind and water, and some are **nonrenewable**, such as the **fossil fuels coal** and **oil**.

As the world's population grows, people are using more water, which creates water shortages, and are causing water **pollution**. We are using more nonrenewable resources too, which are usually mined from the earth and then burned, causing **habitat** destruction and air pollution. People cannot continue to live and act the way they do now—this way of life is unsustainable.

What Is an Environmental Footprint?

A person's environmental footprint describes how much damage that person does to the environment and how quickly the person uses up Earth's resources. A person who protects the environment and does not waste resources has a light environmental footprint. A person who pollutes the environment and wastes resources has a heavy environmental footprint.

Clothing

The clothes we choose to buy have an impact on the environment. Understanding these environmental effects can help us choose "greener" clothing and live more sustainably.

How Clothing Affects the Environment

The clothes you wear affect the environment starting from the time the **fabric** is made and continuing to the point at which the clothes are worn and washed. Often, lots of water and chemicals are used to create fabric, and this uses up natural resources and pollutes the environment. The energy needed to **manufacture**, package, transport, and clean clothing is often created by burning fossil fuels. This harms the environment and is not a sustainable source of energy.

Where to Next?

• To find out how the production, packaging, transport, and cleaning of clothes affects the environment, go to the "Background Briefing" section on page 6.
• To try out fun projects that will help you reduce your environmental footprint, go to the "Living Green Projects" section on page 16.

How Does Buying a Cotton T-Shirt Affect the Environment?

The T-shirt you are wearing may have been made in a factory on another continent, then been shipped to a store in your neighborhood before finiding a place in your home. The journey of that T-shirt may have had a bad effect on the environment.

Growing Cotton

It takes a lot of water to grow cotton. Harmful chemicals are often used, as well.

Making the Fabric

Spinning and weaving cotton uses energy. Most electrical energy is generated by fossil fuels.
The chemicals used in factories can pollute the environment.

Manufacturing the T-Shirt

Sewing machines in clothing factories use energy.

Packaging the T-Shirt

Packaging uses up natural resources and may use nonrenewable materials.

Transporting the T-Shirt to the Store

Planes and trucks burn fossil fuels.

Cleaning the T-Shirt

Washing clothes uses energy and water, and **detergents** can cause water pollution.

Making Fabric

Your clothes are made from different fabrics, which are woven from fibers. Producing fibers and making them into fabric can damage the environment and use up natural resources.

The Environmental Impacts of Making Fabric

Fabric can be made from natural or **artificial fibers**. Artificial fibers are made from nonrenewable resources, so they are not sustainable. Mining the materials used to make artificial fabric harms the Earth. Turning fibers into fabric uses lots of water and electrical energy. This uses up natural resources. Making fabric also uses **toxic** chemicals that pollute and harm the environment.

Natural fibers from cotton bushes are harvested and spun into cotton cloth. Often, growing cotton uses large amounts of water and poisonous chemicals.

Weaving machines in factories use large amounts of electricity. Most electricity is generated by burning fossil fuels.

Natural Fibers Versus Artificial Fibers

Artificial fibers are created in factories using raw materials, such as oil, that are mined from the ground. Nylon, polyester, and acrylic are examples of artificial fibers. **Natural fibers** are fibers that come from animals or plants, such as wool from sheep and cotton from cotton bushes. The most sustainable types of fabric are made from natural fibers grown without artificial **fertilizers** or **pesticides**, and that are not bleached and are dyed using **nontoxic** dyes.

Producing Fibers and Making Fabric

This flowchart shows the main processes involved in making fabric, and the effects these processes have on the environment.

Making Fabric from Artificial Fibers	Making Fabric from Natural Fibers

Mine the Raw Materials

- The raw materials come from nonrenewable sources.
- Mining uses a lot of energy. It can also destroy habitats and create pollution.

Grow Plants or Raise Animals to Produce the Fibers

- Fertilizers can pollute water sources.
- Pesticides can kill helpful insects.
- **Irrigation** can create water shortages.

Turn the Materials into Artificial Fibers

High temperatures are needed to combine the materials and create artificial fibers. This uses a lot of energy.

Untangle, Clean, and Dry the Fibers

A lot of water and energy are used.

Spin the Fibers into Thread and Weave it into Cloth

Spinning and weaving machines use energy.

Bleach, Dye, and Finish the Cloth

Bleaches, dyes, and finishing agents are toxic. They can leak out of the factory, polluting streams and rivers.

7

Manufacturing Clothes

After fabric is made, it is sent to a factory — sometimes in a different country — where it is made into clothes. Manufacturing clothes has its own set of environmental impacts.

The Environmental Impacts of Manufacturing Clothes

Most clothes are not manufactured in a sustainable way. Fabric often needs to be transported a long way to clothing factories, and the machines in clothing factories use a lot of electricity. Most of this electricity is generated by burning fossil fuels, which harms the environment and is not sustainable. The manufactured clothes undergo treatments that complete the look of the clothes. These treatments use a lot of water and can pollute the environment.

Factory workers use electrical sewing machines to sew pieces of fabric together. Most electricity is generated by burning fossil fuels, which has a negative impact on the environment.

Manufacturing Clothes in a Factory

This flowchart shows the main steps involved in manufacturing clothes.

A designer creates the piece of clothing on a computer.
A machine cuts out pattern pieces.
Spreading machines stack the fabric.
Pattern pieces are fastened to the fabric.

Machines cut out the pieces of fabric.
Sewing machine operators sew the pieces of fabric together.
The clothing is pressed and decorations are added. If necessary, they are also washed and chemicals are applied.
The clothes are checked to make sure they are properly sewn.

Transporting the Fabric to the Clothing Factory

The factory where the clothes are made may be in a different city, country, or even continent than the place where the fabric was manufactured. The trucks, trains, boats, or airplanes used to transport the fabric run on fuels made from petroleum, a fossil fuel.

Special Treatments for Clothes

Clothes are sometimes given special treatments before they leave a factory. Different treatments have different purposes and different environmental impacts.

Special Treatments for Clothes

Treatment	Purpose	Environmental Impact
Washing	To remove dye and lighten the color	Uses a lot of water
Applying chemicals	To make the clothes: • look worn • feel softer • wrinkle-free • flameproof	Contributes to water pollution

ECO FACT

Some pieces of clothing are marked with an "ecolabel" that explains how the manufacturer has made the clothing sustainable. The International Organization for Standardization (ISO) is developing an international labeling system for clothing that is manufactured sustainably.

Your clothes are washed before they even get dirty! Clothes are often washed before they leave a factory. Washing clothes uses lots of water and can cause water pollution.

Packaging and Transporting Clothes

Once clothes have been manufactured, they are packaged and transported to clothing stores. When you buy clothes in a store, they are often placed into a plastic bag — even more packaging!

Some clothes, come with a lot of packaging. Not all of the packaging can be recycled.

The Environmental Impacts of Packaging and Transporting Clothes

Many clothes are packaged before they are sent to stores to be sold, and they are often put into yet another bag when sold. Packaging wastes natural resources and it usually becomes **landfill**.

Clothing manufacturers transport and sell their clothes all over the world. Transporting clothes involves burning a lot of fossil fuel, which harms the environment and uses up resources.

Packaging Clothes

Clothes are commonly packaged in cardboard, tissue paper, and plastic. In most cases, this packaging is unnecessary. This wastes resources, and if these materials are not **recycled**, the discarded packaging becomes landfill.

ECO FACT

Some plastic clothes packaging is made from PVC (polyvinyl chloride), which is a type of plastic used around the world because it is cheap and long-lasting. Burning PVC releases toxic gases that can cause health problems for animals and humans.

Transporting Clothes Around the World

Clothes may be taken from the factory by truck to a port, where they are loaded onto a container ship. When the ship reaches its destination, the clothes are loaded onto trucks, which take the clothes to the stores where they will be sold. Ships and trucks run on fossil fuels, so they use up natural resources. They also release **carbon dioxide**, which is linked to **global warming**. The more carbon dioxide a vehicle produces, the more it harms the environment.

Transportation Vehicles and the Amount of Carbon Dioxide They Release

Transportation vehicle	Carbon dioxide (ounces/grams) released when carrying 1 ton of food over 0.6 mile (1 kilometer)
Train 	1.5–2 ounces (39–48 grams)
Ship 	1.5–2 ounces (40–60 grams)
Truck 	7–10 ounces (207–280 grams)
Airplane 	40–75 ounces (1,160–2,150 grams)

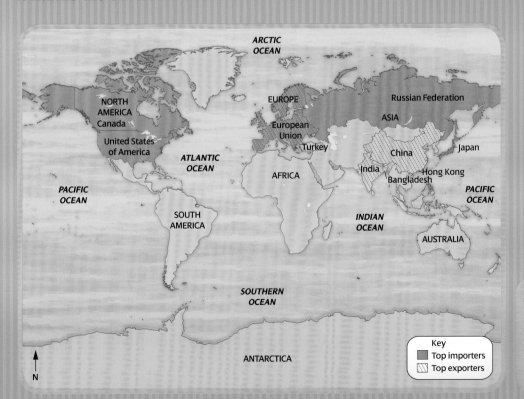

*This map shows the top six **importers** of clothing and the top six **exporters** of clothing in 2011. Transporting clothing long distances has negative environmental impacts.*

Cleaning Clothes

Your clothes have an environmental impact even after you have bought them. When you wear your clothes, you get them dirty and they need to be cleaned. Washing and drying clothes can affect the environment in many ways.

causes pollution

uses water

uses electrical energy

Using a washing machine is an easy way to wash clothes, but it has three major impacts on the environment.

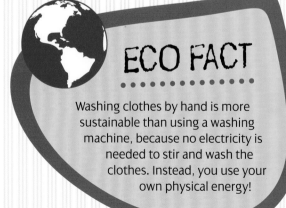

ECO FACT

Washing clothes by hand is more sustainable than using a washing machine, because no electricity is needed to stir and wash the clothes. Instead, you use your own physical energy!

The Environmental Impacts of Cleaning Clothes

Washing clothes in a washing machine has an impact on the environment because the machine uses lots of water and electrical energy, and washing detergents that are rinsed away can cause pollution. Drying clothes in a tumble dryer uses lots of electrical energy, and dry-cleaning uses chemicals that harm the environment.

Washing Clothes in a Washing Machine

Washing machines have three major impacts on the environment:
- They use up to 26 gallons (100 liters) of water per load. Water is a limited resource and washing machines use it up.
- The machines use electrical energy to heat the water and rotate the clothes. Most electricity is generated by burning fossil fuels. This harms the environment and is not sustainable.
- Most laundry detergents contain chemicals made from oil. They are rinsed down the drain and eventually reach rivers and oceans. The chemicals are harmful to marine plants and animals.

Drying Clothes

Tumble dryers are a popular way of drying clothes, but they use a lot of electrical energy. The most sustainable way to dry clothes is to hang them on a line, either indoors or outside.

ECO FACT

Different electrical appliances have different power ratings, which are measured in watts (w) or kilowatts (kw). One kilowatt hour (1 kwh) is the amount of energy that an appliance with a power of 1 kilowatt uses during one hour. The more energy an appliance uses, the greater its environmental impact.

Electrical Energy Needed to Dry One Load of Laundry in Different Ways

Drying Method		Electrical Energy Used (kilowatt hours, kwh)
Tumble drying		4.9 kwh
Dehumidifier		2.1 kwh
Heated drying rack		1.5 kwh
Line drying		0 kwh

Drying a load of laundry on a line uses no electrical energy, so it is a sustainable choice.

Dry Cleaning

Some dry cleaning methods use harmful chemicals. Small amounts of these chemicals are left behind on clothes that have been dry cleaned, and breathing them in can cause health problems. Waste materials from dry cleaning, such as plastic coat hangers and coverings, become landfill.

What Can You Do?

Making green choices when buying clothes can help protect Earth and our future.

You can do many things to reduce the environmental impact of the clothes you wear. Start with making sustainable choices when you buy and clean clothes.

Green Tips for Buying Clothes

Choose clothes that:

✓ are made from natural fibers that were grown without pesticides and fertilizers or that are made from recycled materials

✓ have little or no packaging

✓ are secondhand or vintage

✓ were made in the country where you live

Avoid clothes that:

✗ have loose stitching and could wear out quickly

✗ need to be dry-cleaned

✗ cannot be washed in cold water

Green Tips for Cleaning Clothes

To save both water and energy:

✓ wait until you have a full load before using the washing machine

To save energy:

✓ wash your clothes on the cold temperature setting

✓ hang your clothes outside to dry

To reduce pollution:

✓ use environmentally friendly laundry **detergent**

Green Tips for Clothes You Already Own

✔ Re-purpose the clothes you already have.

✔ Take old clothes to a local thrift store or recycling center.

✔ Organize a clothing "swap meet" with friends.

Local thrift stores are a great way of disposing of unwanted clothes and getting new clothes. Shopping for one-of-a-kind clothing is lots of fun, too!

Living Green Ratings and Green Tips

Pages 16–29 are filled with fun projects that will help you reuse and re-purpose the clothes in your wardrobe and protect Earth from waste and pollution.

Each project is given its own Living Green star rating—from zero to five—as a measurement of how much the project lightens your environmental footprint.

Some projects give Green Tips telling you how you can improve the project's Living Green rating even more.

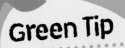

Green Tip

To improve the Living Green rating, make the strap from an old belt or a bicycle inner tube.

On each project spread, look for the Living Green rating. Five stars is the highest—and greenest—rating!

Living Green Rating
★★★★★

★★★	★★★★	★★★★★
A three-star project will teach you about an issue and explain how you are wasting natural resources or causing pollution.	A four-star project will show one or two ways to reduce garbage or pollution.	A five-star project will help you reduce garbage and pollution and actively protect the environment in many different ways.

Refashion a T-Shirt

Give new life to old clothes

Giving new life to old clothes is more sustainable than buying new clothes. When your favorite printed T-shirt becomes stained, out of shape, or worn out, don't throw it away! Use it to redecorate a plain T-shirt.

Living Green Rating

- Reduces the need to buy new clothes, so the environmental impact is smaller
- Reduces landfill, because the old T-shirt is not thrown out

What You Need

- Favorite T-shirt
- Plain T-shirt
- Pinking shears or scissors
- Iron-on interfacing
- Iron
- Needle
- Thread
- Sewing pins

What to Do

1. Choose a large piece of the printed T-shirt that is not stained or worn out. Cut out a piece using pinking shears or scissors.

2. Pin this large patch to the iron-on interfacing. Make sure the sticky side of the interfacing is against the back of the patch.

3. Cut around the edges of the patch.

Green Tip

Make sure that the fabric patch can be washed in the same type of wash cycle as the T-shirt you are adding it to. You don't want the patch to shrink in the wash.

Don't always buy new clothes. Reuse your old or worn-out clothes and make one-of-a-kind outfits!

4. Iron the interfacing to the patch, and then remove the pins. The interfacing will stop the patch from fraying.

5. Pin the patch to the front of the plain T-shirt.

Only use an iron under adult supervision ⚠

6. Hand sew the patch to the T-shirt.

7. Remove the pins and try on your new T-shirt!

Reusing Old Clothes

Repairing, altering, and refashioning your clothes will mean that your clothes last for much longer—and you'll have some one-of-a-kind items.

• Mend rips or holes by covering them with a patch.
• If your pants get too short, add fabric to make them longer or turn them into shorts.
• Use old clothes to make a new item—for example, make a banner from an old sports shirt.
• Give old clothing a new look by dyeing it (see pages 20–23), adding a design using nontoxic fabric paints, sewing on ribbons or sequins, or replacing the buttons.

Upgrade to Arm Warmers

Transform an old sweater into new arm warmers

One way to stay fashionable without buying new clothes is to transform old clothes into new ones. Dress like actress Kristen Stewart, and make your own arm warmers from an old sweater.

Living Green Rating

★ ★ ★ ★ ★

- Reduces the need to buy new clothes, so the environmental impact is smaller
- Reduces landfill, because the old sweater is not thrown out
- Reduces the need for electrical heating, because the arm warmers keep your arms and hands warm

What You Need

- Old woolen sweater
- Measuring tape or ruler
- Pen
- Paper
- Needle
- Thread
- Scissors

What to Do

1. Measure the distance from your elbow to your knuckles. Add 0.5 inch (1.5 centimeters) and then write the measurement down.

2. Cut both sleeves off the sweater.

Find an old woolen sweater and turn it into stylish arm warmers.

3. Starting from the cuff of one sleeve, measure the distance that you recorded in step one. Mark this with a pin and then cut the sleeve there.

4. Turn the sleeve inside out. At the edge you just cut, fold the material over 0.2 inch (0.5 cm) and then fold it again another 0.5 inch (1 cm). Pin the edge.

5. Hand sew this hem.

6. Turn the arm warmer right-side out. Try it on and decide where the thumbhole should be. Mark this place with a pin.

7. Use the scissors to cut a small slit at the place you marked.

8. Turn the arm warmer inside out. Sew around the edges of the thumbhole so that it won't fray.

9. Repeat steps three to eight to make the second arm warmer.

Green Tip

You could also make arm warmers from old socks that have holes in their toes.

Dyeing for a Change

Use plants and food to dye your clothes

Most store-bought dyes are made from toxic chemicals, so they are not good for the environment. But you can make your own natural dyes from nontoxic plant materials.

Living Green Rating
★ ★ ★ ★

• Reduces the need to buy new clothes, so the environmental impact is smaller
• Uses natural dyes, so no toxic chemicals are released to pollute the water system

What You Need

• Piece of cotton clothing, such as a tank top or T-shirt
• Plant materials (see table below)
• Large saucepan
• Vinegar
• Salt
• Measuring pitcher
• Mixing bowl
• Knife
• Chopping block
• Rubber gloves

What to Do

1. First, you need to make a special solution that will prepare the fabric so that the dye works well. For most plant materials, mix 1 part vinegar with 4 parts cold water. If using berries, mix 1 part salt with 16 parts cold water. Use the measuring pitcher and mix in a bowl.

2. Half-fill the saucepan with the mixture, and put the top into the pan.

Plant Materials That Can Be Used as Dyes

Color of Dye	Plant Materials
Pink or red	Strawberries, cherries, raspberries
Orange	Carrots, lilac twigs, onion skins
Yellow	Marigolds, dandelions
Green	Spinach leaves, lilac flowers, snapdragons
Blue or purple	Red cabbage, blackberries, blueberries
Brown	Tea bags, coffee grounds, dandelion roots

Look in your garden or kitchen for plant materials that can be used to make natural dyes.

3. Place the saucepan on the stove and simmer for one hour.

4. Take the saucepan off the heat and leave to cool.

5. Empty the saucepan and rinse the top in cold water.

6. Chop up the plant material.

7. Place the plant material in the saucepan. Add twice the volume of cold water as there is plant material.

Only use the stove with adult supervision

8. Place the top in the saucepan. Simmer on the stove until you get the right color. Remember, the color will lighten as the top dries.

9. Remove the saucepan from the heat and leave to cool.

10. Wearing rubber gloves, remove the top from the pan.

11. Rinse the top in cold water, then hang on the line to dry.

Green Tip

For best results, dye white or light-colored clothes made from natural fibers.

Color Transformation

Transform an old T-shirt by tie-dyeing it

Once you know how to make natural dyes (see pages 20–21), you can start to experiment with color. Transform an old, boring T-shirt by adding a colorful pattern.

What You Need

• White cotton T-shirt
• Plant materials to make the dye (see page 20)
• Large saucepan
• Vinegar
• Salt
• Measuring pitcher
• Mixing bowl
• Knife
• Chopping block
• Rubber gloves
• Rubber bands or string

What to Do

1. Follow steps one to seven on pages 20–21.

2. Fold and tie the T-shirt to create the pattern you want (see table on page 23).

3. Follow steps eight to eleven on page 21. Untie the T-shirt before rinsing it in step 11.

You can use natural dyes to create different patterns and effects.

How To Create Different Patterns

Pattern	What to Do	Result
Marbled Crumple the T-shirt and tie it many times to get this effect.		
Spiral Swirl the T-shirt and tie it four times to get this effect.		
Stripes Roll the T-shirt and tie up the roll to create stripes.		

Experiment More

Experiment more with color and fabrics. Try various ways of folding, twisting, and pinching the fabric, and place the rubber bands or string in different places. Try dyeing multicolored fabrics or cotton clothing that has stitching made from artificial fibers. The stitching will not absorb the dye, resulting in a different pattern.

Recycled Bracelet

Turn a toothbrush into a fashion statement!

Most store-bought jewelry is not manufactured sustainably. By turning an old toothbrush into a colorful bracelet, you'll reduce your environmental impact—and no one else will have your style!

Living Green Rating

⭐ ⭐ ⭐ ⭐

- Reduces the need to buy new jewelry, so the environmental impact is smaller
- Reduces landfill, because the old toothbrush is not thrown out as garbage

What You Need

- An old toothbrush
- Tweezers
- Tongs
- Bowl
- Mug
- Oven gloves
- Kitchen towel
- 2 cups boiling water
- 1 cup cold water

What to Do

1. Use the tweezers to remove the bristles from the toothbrush.

2. Pour the boiling water into the bowl.

3. Use the tongs to put the toothbrush into the bowl of boiling water. Leave for 5 minutes.

Take care! Boiling water can burn you! ⚠

4. Use the tongs to remove the toothbrush from the bowl. Place it on a towel.

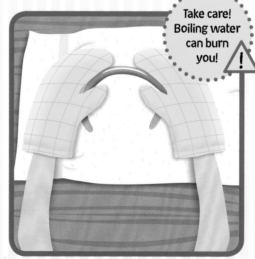

5. Wearing the oven gloves, bend the toothbrush into a bracelet shape.

Create one-of-a-kind jewelry using your old, scruffy toothbrush!

6. Put the bent toothbrush into the mug. The sides of the mug will stop the toothbrush from uncurling as it cools.

7. Pour the cold water into the mug. Leave the toothbrush to cool for a few minutes.

8. Wear your bracelet as it is or decorate it using one of the ideas below.

Decorating Your Bracelet

Decorate your bracelet by:
- using a metallic felt-tip pen to add your name or the name of a sports team you like
- gluing on sequins, glitter, or shiny paper
- tieing on old beads using thin thread

Green Tip

Make different kinds of bracelets using these waste materials:
- odd buttons threaded onto sewing thread
- old shoelaces
- scraps of ribbon
- safety pins joined together

Brand New Knapsack

Refashion a T-shirt into a knapsack

One way to live more sustainably is by turning old clothes into new accessories. For this project, you can reuse an old T-shirt to make a stylish knapsack that looks as good as new.

Living Green Rating

★ ★ ★ ★ ★

- Reduces the need to buy a new bag, so the environmental impact is smaller
- If shopping, reduces the need to use a plastic bag, so less environmental impact
- Reduces landfill, because the old T-shirt is not thrown out as garbage

What You Need

- Old T-shirt
- Scissors
- Sewing machine
- Needle
- Thread
- Sewing pins
- About 1.5 feet (50 cm) of strap
- About 2.5 feet (80 cm) of cord
- Safety pin

What to Do

1. Turn the T-shirt inside out and lay it flat.

2. Cut off both sleeves.

3. Cut the neck off in a straight line.

4. In one of the cut corners, pin and hand sew the end of the strap to the top layer of the T-shirt.

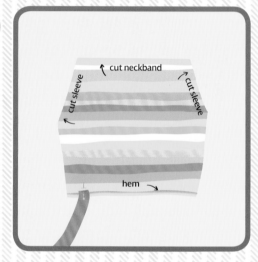

5. Tuck the strap between the two layers of the T-shirt. Keep the strap flat and untwisted.

You can use a little imagination and a sewing machine to turn a T-shirt into a new knapsack.

6. Pin the other end of the strap to the opposite corner. Again, pin it to the top layer of the T-shirt.

7. Hand sew the strap to the T-shirt.

8. Pin together the three cut sides of the T-shirt. Sew around the sides using the sewing machine. Do this twice.

Ask an adult for help with the sewing machine ⚠️

9. Turn the T-shirt right side out.

10. At the top of the knapsack, roll the hem between your fingers to separate the two layers. Cut two small slits in the hem, about 0.75 inches (2 cm) apart.

11. Attach a safety pin to one end of the cord and thread the pin and the cord through the hem. Remove the safety pin and tie a large knot in each end of the cord.

12. Try out your new knapsack!

Green Tip

To improve the Living Green rating, make the strap from an old belt or a bicycle inner tube.

Living Green Projects

Living Green Rating

★ ★ ★ ★

- Reduces the need to buy detergent and fabric softener, so the environmental impact is smaller
- Uses natural ingredients, so no toxic chemicals are released to pollute the water system

What You Need

- Bar of laundry soap
- 1 cup **baking soda**
- 1 cup borax
- Large bowl
- Rubber spatula
- Grater
- Plate
- Container with lid

Green Clean

Make your own detergent and fabric softener

Homemade laundry detergents and fabric softeners are much kinder to the environment than most store-bought versions. They also cost a fraction of the price and are easy to make!

Laundry Detergent

What to Do

1. Grate the bar of soap onto a plate. Use the fine side of the grater.

2. Add the grated soap to the bowl, and then add the baking soda and borax.

3. Mix well, using the rubber spatula.

4. Put the detergent in the container and make sure the lid is fastened tightly.

5. Use 2 tablespoons of detergent per load of laundry.

Keep your clothes fresh, clean, and good for the environment by washing them in homemade detergent.

Fabric Softener

What You Need

- 4 cups water
- 2 cups white vinegar
- 2 cups baking soda
- Large bowl
- Rubber spatula
- Container with lid

What to Do

1. Pour the water and vinegar into the bowl.

2. Add the baking soda a little at a time. The mixture will fizz.

3. Stir well.

4. Store in the container with the lid tightly fastened.

5. Shake the mixture and add a quarter cup to your washing machine for the final rinse.

Label your containers of detergent and fabric softener and keep them out of reach of babies and young children !

Green Tip

To make your clothes smell fresh, add two or three drops of lavender or eucalyptus oil to your homemade fabric softener.

Find Out More About Living Green

The Internet is a great way of finding out more about the environmental impact of clothes and what you can do to make more sustainable clothing choices.

Useful Websites

Visit these useful websites:

🖱 http://diyfashion.about.com/od/recycledprojects/tp/Recycle-Your-Clothes.htm
This page suggests various ways of turning old clothes into new fashion items.

🖱 http://unep.org/tunza/children
This website from the United Nations has downloadable fact sheets about environmental issues, tips for living more sustainably, and competitions you can enter.

🖱 www.wikihow.com/Recycle-Your-Socks
This page has lots of fun ideas for reusing old socks.

Searching for Information

Here are some terms you might enter into your Internet search bar find out more about clothing and sustainability:
• environmental impact of clothing
• cotton and pesticides
• organic cotton
• recycled fabric
• wardrobe refashion

Glossary

artificial fibers Fibers that are made by people and do not come directly from nature.

baking soda White, powdery chemical compound used for cooking and cleaning; also called sodium bicarbonate or bicarb soda.

carbon dioxide A greenhouse gas that is released when fossil fuels are burned, for example when coal is burned to make electricity.

detergents Liquid or powder cleaning materials that clean away dirt and oil.

environment The natural world, including plants, animals, land, rivers, and oceans.

exporters Countries that send products to another country for sale.

fabric Cloth produced by weaving or knitting fibers together.

fertilizers Substances added to the soil to help crops grow better.

fossil fuels Coal, oil, and natural gas, which are natural resources that are formed from the remains of dead plants and animals, deep under Earth's surface, over millions of years.

global warming The process by which Earth's average temperature is getting warmer.

habitat Place where plants and animals live.

importers Countries that bring in products from another country.

irrigation Supplying water to a dry area to help crops grow.

landfill Garbage that is buried and covered with soil at garbage dumps.

manufacture Make from raw materials into a product for people to buy and use.

natural fibers Fibers from plants and animals, such as cotton and wool, which can be spun and woven into cloth.

natural resources Natural materials that can be used by humans, such as wood, metal, coal, and water.

nonrenewable resources Natural resources that cannot be easily replaced, such as coal, oil, and natural gas.

nontoxic Not poisonous to living things.

oil A liquid found in rocks, formed from the remains of plants and animals that lived millions of years ago.

pesticides Poisonous chemicals used to prevent pests, such as insects, fungi, and weeds, from damaging crops by killing the pests.

pollution Damaging substances, especially chemicals or waste products, that harm the environment.

recycled Having treated the materials contained in a product so that they can be used again.

renewable resources Natural resources that will never run out, such as the wind, or that can easily be replaced, such as wood.

toxic Poisonous to living things.

Index